LOVE HAIKU
Masajo Suzuki

Translations by
Lee Gurga and Emiko Miyashita

LOVE HAIKU

Masajo Suzuki's Lifetime of Love

Translations by
Lee Gurga and Emiko Miyashita

Introduction by Patricia Donegan
with Yoshie Ishibashi

Brooks Books
Decatur, Illinois

ACKNOWLEDGMENTS

The translators would like to express their appreciation to Dr. Akito Arima for guiding Emiko into this haiku world, realizing the 2nd HIA-HSA Conference in Tokyo in 1997, and opening Emiko's eyes to the English haiku community and Lee's eyes to the richness of contemporary Japanese haiku; Shizuo Abe for taking Emiko to *Unami* and introducing her to Masajo in 1995; Emiko's husband Susumu Miyashita, and her children Manabu and Sai, for their warmest support at home; Lee's wife Jan and his children Ben, A.J., and Alex for their understanding during the continued mental absence of their husband and father during work on this book; Yukio Hanawa, the general manager of Kamogawa Grand Hotel, for his kindness and consideration during our visit there, where we were able to hear the same surf that Masajo had heard and breathe the same sea air that Masajo had breathed; Teruko Suzuki, Masajo's stepdaughter, and Muneo Imada, Masajo's grandson, for their hospitality when we visited *Unami* in September, 1999; Randy Brooks for his kind offer to design and publish this book; Pat Donegan and Yoshie Ishibashi for their enthusiastic interest in Masajo's work; Lidia Rozmus for her encouragement and wise counsel; Jane Reichhold for permission to use quotes on Masajo from her web site; David Burleigh for reviewing the introductions; Fay Aoyagi for her penetrating comments on some of the translations; Keikin Katayama for her model calligraphy for Emiko. And finally we would like to thank Masajo for her love haiku, for her permission to translate them and publish them in English, and for the time she shared with Emiko in Ginza.

Some of these translations appeared previously in *Modern Haiku*.

First Edition • ISBN: 1-929820-00-3

Brooks Books
4634 Hale Drive
Decatur, IL 62526

http://www.family-net.net/~brooksbooks

鈴木真砂女

Introduction

by
Patricia Donegan with Yoshie Ishibashi

> firefly light:
> I step off the path
> of woman's virtue

Masajo Suzuki followed her own path. She is not just a love
poet in the sense of writing about her lover and love relation-
ship, but a love poet in the larger sense of loving life and
living it fully. She is a poet who has lived life devoted to her
art, writing about her everyday life, whether a sensual haiku
about lying with her lover in the grass:

> firefly finds his love
> they settle into grass
> together

or a mundane haiku about her pub's dinner:

> steamed in sake—
> small clams open their shells
> the night's coldness

(from the *Imachizuki* collection). All her haiku are imbued
with passion, a passionate sense for living. She herself said
she lived for haiku, her lover and her pub—these three
aspects of her life embody her strong spirit to feast on
loving life.

This vision of love is reflected in Masajo Suzuki's *Love Haiku,*
co-translated by Lee Gurga and Emiko Miyashita. These love
haiku were carefully selected and edited by the translation
team, out of a larger canon of mostly traditional haiku (writ-
ten from 1936-1998). These finely selected and translated love
haiku represent one of the few books devoted to a single
woman haiku poet. If only this book had been available
twenty years ago, when some of us were experimenting with
love haiku and were ignorant that Masajo and other modern
Japanese women poets had been writing love haiku for half a
century or more. At that time, there was a scarcity of transla-
tions in English; one rare source was Akiko Yosano's erotic
tanka poetry, and some other women's haiku were scattered
in various anthologies. There are still many women haiku
poets whose work needs to be translated. Especially great
women haiku masters of the twentieth century like Kanajo
Hasegawa, Hisajo Sugita, Takako Hashimoto, Teijo
Nakamura, and Nobuko Katsura, to name some major voices.
Hopefully, this team will continue to co-translate some of
these other women poets. For the luminosity of language in
these sparse translations conveys the subtle beauty and
strength of Masajo's original haiku—and that is an achieve-
ment.

The theme of love, traditionally in Japan, was reserved for
waka (tanka) poetry—this form was for centuries dominated
by courtesan women and used subjective emotional expres-
sion. However, the much later haiku form was initially
thought to be a male form of literature because it was more
objective and emphasized nature as its theme. It took some
early twentieth century poets to expand the tradition-bound
haiku form to include more subjective elements of love and
sensuality. This approach to haiku can be found here and
there through the centuries, even in some of Basho's haiku
(*hokku*). However, except for some of his verses written as
part of the *renga* (linked verse form) which included 'love
verses', he didn't write individual love haiku in the modern

sense. That was left to modern times, to the women poet forerunners like Hisajo Sugita, Takako Hashimoto and the rare male poets like Kusatao Nakamura and Sojo Hino, and, a little later, to Masajo Suzuki.

Few haiku poets express the theme of love as directly and consistently as Masajo, as if looking into the diary of her love life, or into human beings' deepest desire. Masajo's haiku not only share her vision of love, but expand our perception of haiku, so that it can include any life experience and can express not just the Zen-like moments in nature 'of being one with the frog' but also the moments 'of being one with love', as these examples of her haiku show: of finding the kimono sash of one's lover in an old chest, longing for love while eating a strawberry, the loneliness of love amidst crickets in the dark, and the thought of love's betrayal on hearing the shrike's cry. Each haiku is a mini-drama of her life, because it was from her real experience, a mirror of her life.

It is interesting that Masajo chose to use haiku rather than tanka or free verse forms to express the theme of love; for there were other pre-war and post-war poets writing love tanka and free verse love poems. Masajo and other haiku poets writing 'love haiku' retained the basic haiku form because they still kept the tradition of the *kigo* or seasonal reference (that some other modern haiku poets had rejected), using the basic 'sketch of nature' approach. But they expanded the haiku form, by adding the imagery and feeling of love, making 'love haiku'. It is as if Masajo's heart is the center of her haiku and the *kigo* is used to surround it. Although she writes with exquisite objective imagery, it is dyed in her feelings as if she is writing on white paper that has been soaked in hues of red:

> a fallen camellia:
> vivid vivid crimson
> it remains

or

midwinter rouge—
my heart's darkness
cannot be discerned

or

withered grass
when I think of him …
burnished gold

or

the last drop
from the perfume bottle—
cherry blossom rain

If Masajo's love haiku were somewhat of a sensation in her time it was because her lifestyle itself was unusual, for she was not a courtesan or mistress, but a wife and later a divorced woman who was openly having a love affair with a married man, and writing about it openly. In her time, the living of it would have been more objectionable than the writing of it. For in her era, especially of post-war Japan, women had to be in the role of the good wife and mother, embracing the virtues of modesty and selflessness. Masajo's haiku were against convention and recorded her life honestly—living freely in the face of strict traditions. In the midst of the flurry of love and the busyness of running her pub, the discipline of writing haiku every night in her room, after her pub closed, became her solace and the back-bone of her life. It was through haiku that she found a way to celebrate the sacredness of love and of life itself.

Masajo became one of Japan's best known haiku love poets of modern times because she wasn't afraid to be herself and follow her own path. She courageously took her intensely lived experiences—be they longing for love or just cooking a seasonal dish—and put them into the haiku form, compressing these moments into one breath, a love sigh on paper. We can almost hear her voice through these translations, as if Masajo herself is whispering them for the first time to her lover, or just reciting them alone in reminiscence to the silent night air, while sipping sake in her pub on a winter night in Tokyo.

winter mist—
memories of embracing
and being embraced

Translators' Introduction

"I have been in love at all the times." So says Masajo Suzuki, premier love haiku poet of contemporary Japanese haiku. Masajo (whose real name is Masa Suzuki) was born in 1906 as the third daughter of the owner of a seaside resort hotel, *Yoshidaya*, at Kamogawa. She married in 1929 and had a daughter, Kakuko (1932-), but divorced later due to her husband's mysterious disappearance in 1935. In the same year, her elder sister, Ryû, died suddenly leaving her four children. So Masajo had to take over management of the hotel and was obligated to marry her dead sister's husband at the age of thirty.

Masajo met her destined love, Y.M. (1913-1977), in 1936. As an officer of naval air force, Y.M. took his crew to stay in her hotel for a weekend. This tall, handsome naval aviator was seven years younger than Masajo. The following weekend, he came alone, while Masajo's husband was away in Tokyo. Their love continued for forty years until Y.M.'s death in 1977.

Y.M. and haiku both came into Masajo's life in the same period. She met the haiku poets with whom her sister had been involved at her funeral. Ryû had been a haiku poet (her haiku name was Ryûjo), and Masajo gradually understood the magic of haiku that had attracted her sister so much. Haiku enabled Masajo to open up a world in which she could be free and creative, unlike the one in which she was living with a husband she could not love. She began studying haiku under the guidance of her late sister's master, Hakusuirô Ôba, in 1936. She subsequently joined the *Shuntô* (Light of Spring Night) haiku group and studied under the guidance of Mantarô Kubota until his death in 1963.

In 1938, Y.M. was transferred to a base at Ômura in Kyûshû and Masajo became aware that he was going to be sent to war in two weeks. Though she was still married, Masajo without hesitation took a train to be with him. They stayed in a hotel together for just these two weeks. During the day, Y.M. worked at the base and returned to Masajo in the evening. After this short time together, Y.M. left for the war and Masajo returned to Kamogawa. Later, in 1941, Y.M. was sent back to Japan suffering from tuberculosis. Masajo went to see him in the hospital, and it was there she was told that he had a wife and two children. She was shocked but her love did not change. He remained hospitalized for the following fourteen years.

In January 1957, Masajo went to Tokyo to see her daughter Kakuko's performance in a drama. That night, a messenger came from her husband, who was aware that she had a lover, and gave Masajo the choice of either returning to the hotel and caring for him, or giving up her claim to ownership of the hotel. She chose to be divorced at once and did not return to Kamogawa. On March 30 of the same year, with her friends' financial support, she opened a tiny pub, *Unami* (April Waves) in Ginza, Tokyo.

When Y.M. was released from the hospital, *Unami* was already running successfully. She found an apartment in Toranomon for their life together, which lasted for about a year. Y.M. usually stayed with Masajo during the week and returned to his family on weekends. But on the weekends he did not return home, he and Masajo often took a taxi and went to see a movie together, hand in hand. "When we are together, we are always holding each other's hands. His big hand covers mine and his fingers move to open my fingers and then to close. How I love it!" Masajo still keeps a tiny piece of bone from Y.M.'s finger that was picked up from his cremation ashes and brought to her by one of his friends.

Of his wife, Masajo said, "I was never jealous of his wife, but when she died and was buried next to him, I felt offended by this!"

Masajo says of love, "Love in my haiku is always vivid and alive. In my heart love does not belong to the past but to NOW. I wrote this haiku when I was eighty-eight years old:"

> shall we die together?
> he whispers in my ear . . .
> fireflies at dusk

When asked about influence on her haiku, Masajo said, "The influence of arts and artists on me have been not small, but what has most influenced my haiku? Love! It has been the source all of my artistic activities."

Her fourth book *Yûboraru* (Evening Fireflies) won the 16th *Haijinkyôkai* Prize in 1976 and in 1995, she won the *Yomiuri* Literature Prize for her sixth book *Miyakodori* (Black-headed Gull). In 1998, her seventh book *Shimokuren* (Purple Magnolia) won the *Dakotsu* Prize, which is considered the highest award in the haiku world.

Emiko: "Without experiencing true love, one can not write a real love haiku." "My lover has been dead for twenty years, but the memories with him are still so vivid—the emotion of true love will last for a lifetime." This is what Masajo told me when I showed her my humble love haiku. Masajo writes of love using everyday language, in contrast to the archaic, literary language used by many haiku poets of her day. Thus her love haiku pierce straight into the hearts of both haiku poets and ordinary people, making her the most popular love haiku poet in Japan. I will never forget the first time I went to *Unami*; her fingers with a pale pink manicure served us the specialty of the pub, fried sardine rolls, so gracefully.

Lee: Emiko and I went to *Unami* together in September, 1999, where we met Pat Donegan and Yoshie Ishibashi, translators of the famous woman haiku master, Chiyo-ni. Masajo's stepdaughter, Teruko, served us dinner. The calligraphy of Mantarô looked down on us from the wall. Each matchbox of the pub had the season's haiku by Masajo printed on it. At the little *Saiwai-Inari* shrine around the corner from the pub, we bowed and clapped our hands in supplication as Masajo had done so many times, seeking blessings for her haiku. The rattle of our coins in the offering box mixed with the voices and sounds of Ginza around us.

Inspired by a love story we heard at the Haiku North America conference in Evanston, Illinois in the summer of 1999, we began translating Masajo's haiku. This book contains 150 love haiku we have translated, selected from the 2,576 haiku in her seven haiku books published between 1955 and 1998. We hope they will touch your hearts as they have touched ours.

Lee Gurga and Emiko Miyashita
Lincoln, Illinois, U.S.A. & Kawasaki, Japan

gurga@ccaonline.com & emikom@msn.com

June 1, 2000

A NOTE ON SEASONAL WORDS

One of the defining elements of haiku is the presence of a seasonal reference that relates one's personal experience to the always changing but ever recurring cycle of the seasons. Since some of the seasonal references in Japanese haiku refer to elements of Japanese culture with which the Western reader would not be familiar, we have decided to make a note of the seasonal word in each haiku.

Contents

IKESUKAGO
(Bamboo Creel)
1955

生れざりせばと思ふとき雁かへる

umarezariseba to omou toki kari kaeru

when I think
I should never have been born—
departing geese

*I was extravagant in my way of living, but never thought it was a happy life.
How many times have I thought of not coming into being?*

Seasonal word: departing geese (spring)

鏡台にぬきし指輪や花の雨

kyôdai ni nukishi yubiwa ya hana no ame

on the dressing table
the ring removed from my finger—
cherry blossom rain

Seasonal word: cherry blossom rain (spring)

坐りたるまゝ帯とくや花疲れ

suwaritaru mama obi toku ya hanazukare

without standing up
I untie my obi—
blossom viewing fatigue

Seasonal word: cherry blossom fatigue (spring)
Note: An *obi* (kimono sash) is usually tied and untied in a standing
position.

春淋し波にとゞかぬ石を投げ

haru sabishi nami ni todokanu ishi wo nage

spring loneliness—
it falls short of the surf
this stone I toss

*When I was filled with loneliness, I often went to the seaside in the mornings
and evenings. With my thin arm I would toss a stone to the rough surf, but the
stone hardly reached it. I felt I was completely helpless and trapped in my
destiny at that time.*

Seasonal word: spring

人 の そ し り 知 つ て の 春 の 愁 ひ か な

hito no soshiri shitte no haru no urei kana

people's censure
I know all about it . . .
sorrow in spring

In a small town people are more concerned about what others are doing. From my hair style to the clothes I wore, I was the target of their curiosity and objections. Being flamboyant for a small town, I took this interest as a matter of course.

Seasonal word: spring sorrow (spring)

あ る と き は 船 よ り 高 き 卯 浪 か な

aru toki wa fune yori takaki unami kana

at one time
rising above the boat . . .
April waves

A little boat is floating on the sea. At one moment it disappears behind a tall wave and comes out again. It is the same in real life, too. One experiences the heights and then the depths, and comes back again.

Seasonal word: April (in the lunar calendar) waves (spring)

夏帯や夫への嫉妬さらになく

natsuobi ya tsuma e no shitto sarani naku

summer obi—
jealous of my husband?
never!

Seasonal word: summer obi (kimono sash) (summer)

火蛾舞へりよき襟あしをもてる人

higa maeri yoki eriashi wo moteru hito

a moth dances into the flame . . .
the nape of the man's neck
draws me in

Seasonal word: moth (summer)

羅や人悲します恋をして

usumono ya hito kanashimasu koi wo shite

sheer summer kimono—
it pushes them into misery
this love of mine

Seasonal word: sheer summer kimono (summer)
Note: When Masajo was 31 years old, she fell in love with one of her
hotel's guests, Air Force Lieutenant Y.M. (1913-1977), then 24 years old.
In those days infidelity was a crime in Japan. Masajo thought of herself
as a sinner and felt sorry for her parents, her husband, her lover, and for
herself. This is among the most popular of her love haiku.

あるときの心のむごく毛虫焼く

aru toki no kokoro no mugoku kemushi yaku

that one time
my heart so merciless:
I burned a hairy caterpillar

Seasonal word: hairy caterpillar (summer)

手をのせし胸の薄さや今朝の秋

te wo noseshi mune no ususa ya kesa no aki

I touched my chest
and felt its thinness—
autumn's first morning

At that time, I weighed less than 40 kilograms (88 pounds). My chest, which had recovered from a mild case of tuberculosis, was thin, but I kept a burning desire in this thin chest.

Seasonal word: autumn's first morning
Note: *Kesa no aki* is the morning of the first day of autumn, which is around August 7th or 8th.

ふところに手紙かくして日向ぼこ

futokoro ni tegami kakushite hinataboko

your letter concealed
in my kimono's breast pocket—
basking in winter sun

Seasonal word: basking in winter sun (winter)

女三界に家なき雪のつもりけり

on'na sangai ni ie naki yuki no tsumori keri

in these three worlds
a woman is never at home;
snow on snow on snow

Seasonal word: snow (winter)
Note: *On'na sangai ni ie nashi* means that there is no home for a woman
to live in peace in the whole world. She must obey her father when she
is a child, humble herself to her husband when she gets married, and
follow her eldest son after the death of her husband.

28

UNAMI
(APRIL WAVES)
1961

卯浪

御身思ふこと如何ばかり雁かへる

onmi omou koto ikabakari kari kaeru

your well being
how much I care . . .
the geese depart

Seasonal word: geese depart (spring)

砂山に人の恋見し日永かな

sunayama ni hito no koi mishi hinaga kana

on the seaside dunes
other people in love . . .
lingering daylight

Seasonal word: lingering daylight (spring)

香水の一ト瓶終り花の雨

kôsui no hitobin owari hana no ame

the last drop
from the perfume bottle—
cherry blossom rain

Seasonal word: cherry blossom rain (spring)

かりそめの夫の座布団花ぐもり

karisome no tsuma no zabuton hanagumori

a zabuton cushion
for my borrowed husband—
cherry blossom clouds

Seasonal word: cherry blossom clouds (spring)
Note: *Zabuton* is a floor cushion to sit on.

すみれ野に罪あるごとく来て二人

sumireno ni tsumi aru gotoku kite futari

field of violets—
like those fallen from grace
like the two of us

Seasonal word: violet (spring)

襟足をみせて髪結ふ新樹かな

eriashi wo misete kami yu'u shinju kana

I put up my hair
so he sees the nape of my neck . . .
new green leaves

Seasonal word: trees in fresh green leaves (summer)

夏帯や運切りひらき切りひらき

natsuobi ya un kirihiraki kirihiraki

summer kimono sash—
my destiny in my hand
in my own hands

*My fortune is something I have to hew out for myself. The only person I can
rely on is myself. I put on my summer kimono sash smartly and just keep
working.*

Seasonal word: summer kimono sash (summer)

蛍火や女の道をふみはづし

hotarubi ya on'na no michi wo fumihazushi

firefly light:
I step off the path
of woman's virtue

*What is a woman's path? Is it to live a life of good wife and wise mother? I have
stepped out from that path. When I am watching the firefly's light going on and
off, I have no idea what will happen to my future.*

Seasonal word: firefly (summer)

ビールくむ抱かるゝことのなき人と

bîru kumu dakaruru koto no naki hito to

a glass of beer—
I serve it to a man
I will never love

Seasonal word: beer (summer)

空の色に見る海の色秋燕

sora no iro ni miru umi no iro akitsubame

in the sky's color
the color of the sea—
autumn swallows

Seasonal word: autumn swallows (autumn)

髪解くや情に溺れし秋の髪

kami toku ya jô ni oboreshi aki no kami

I let my hair down . . .
it is drowning in desire
my autumn hair

Seasonal word: autumn

秋風や知らぬ顔して行きし人

akikaze ya shiranu kao shite yukishi hito

autumn wind—
he pretends not to see me
as he passes

Seasonal word: autumn wind (autumn)

夫運なき秋袷着たりけり

otto un naki akiawase kitari keri

luck with husbands
is something that eludes me—
autumn kimono

*I married twice and divorced twice. My first marriage ended with the
mysterious disappearance of my husband. In the second one, I left the house of
my own will. Since then I have been making my living in a corner of Tokyo.*

Seasonal word: autumn kimono (autumn)

こほろぎや眼を見はれども闇は闇

kôrogi ya me wo miharedomo yami wa yami

crickets—
my eyes wide open to darkness
nothing but darkness

Seasonal word: cricket (autumn)
Note: Masajo is looking for her lover who might come to visit in the
dark. But she sees only the darkness.

人恋し青き木の実を掌にぬくめ

hito koishi aoki konomi wo te ni nukume

longing for him
I warm a green acorn
in my hand

Seasonal word: acorn (autumn)

菊日和身にまく帯の長きかな

kikubiyori mi ni maku obi no nagaki kana

chrysanthemum blooming—
the sash bound round my waist
oh, so long

Seasonal word: chrysanthemums blooming (autumn)

野分中波にのまれてしまひたき

nowaki naka nami ni nomarete shimaitaki

autumn gale—
to be swallowed by a wave
is my wish

Seasonal word: autumn gale (autumn)

男憎しされども恋し柳散る

otoko nikushi saredomo koishi yanagi chiru

I detest the man
yet I long for him—
willow leaves falling

Seasonal word: willow leaves falling (autumn)

水鳥や別れ話は女より

mizutori ya wakarebanashi wa on'na yori

waterbirds —
talk of divorce
from the woman

I tried to talk about divorce once, but failed. As far as I know, it is always from the woman's side to bring up the subject of divorce.

Seasonal word: waterbirds (winter)

誰よりもこの人が好き枯草に

dare yorimo kono hito ga suki karekusa ni

more than anyone
it is this man I love
on the withered grass

Seasonal word: withered grass (winter)

洗髪乾かぬ雪となりにけり

araigami kawakanu yuki to nari ni keri

shampooed hair
remaining damp
it becomes snowy

Seasonal word: snow (winter)

同じ空の下に住む雪つもるかな

onaji sora no shita ni sumu yuki tsumoru kana

under the same sky
your life and my life. . .
snow piles on snow

Seasonal word: snow (winter)
Note: Masajo moved to live in Tokyo, and her lover was in a
sanatorium in a suburb of Tokyo. Masajo looked up in the sky and
thought they were living under the same sky now. Snow was falling
and was covering the ground. She wondered if his place was also
covered with snow.

降る雪やあざやかすぎし夢の虹

furu yuki ya azayaka sugishi yume no niji

falling snow—
too brilliant a rainbow
in my dream

Seasonal word: snow (winter)

凍星のわれをゆるさぬ光かな

iteboshi no ware wo yurusanu hikari kana

frozen star . . .
unforgiving light
falls on me

Seasonal word: frozen star (winter)

口きいてくれず冬濤見てばかり

kuchi kiite kurezu fuyunami mite bakari

not a word for me
he just continues to watch
the winter waves

Seasonal word: winter waves (winter)

NATSUOBI
(SUMMER KIMONO SASH)
1969

旅かなし白梅むしろ青しと見

tabi kanashi hakubai mushiro aoshi to mi

sadness on a journey—
white plum blossoms
I see as blue

Seasonal word: white plum blossoms (spring)

あはれ野火の草あるかぎり狂ひけり

aware nobi no kusa aru kagiri kurui keri

how piteous!
as long as there is grass
the wildfire rages

Seasonal word: wildfire (spring)

淋しさも草を焼く火もひろごりぬ

sabishisa mo kusa wo yaku hi mo hirogorinu

solitude, too
fire burning grass, too
have spread

Seasonal word: burning grass (spring)

落椿生き生きと紅たもちをり

ochi tsubaki iki-iki to beni tamochi wori

a fallen camellia:
vivid vivid crimson
it remains

Seasonal word: fallen camellia (spring)

四月馬鹿髪結ひあげてどこへも出ず

shigatsu baka kami yuiagete doko e mo dezu

April Fool—
I do up my hair and go
nowhere

Seasonal word: April Fool (spring)

またよりをもどせし仲や囀れり

mata yori wo modoseshi naka ya saezureri

the two back
on good terms again—
birds twittering

Seasonal word: birds twittering (spring)

情無しを恨むも愛か木瓜の雨

jônashi wo uramu mo ai ka boke no ame

his cold-heartedness:
shouldn't my love begrudge it?
quince rain

Bearing a grudge against the man and longing for him at the same time, these are what woman's heart does. And it is called love. The crimson of the Japanese quince deepens as it gets wet with rain.

Seasonal word: Japanese quince flower (spring)

匙を逃げし苺ひと粒春うれひ

saji wo nigeshi ichigo hitotsubu haru urei

from the spoon
one strawberry escapes—
spring sorrow

Seasonal word: spring sorrow (spring)

水飲みてふたたびねむり夜半の春

mizu nomite futatabi nemuri yowa no haru

a drink of water
then again to sleep—
a night in spring

Seasonal word: a night in spring (spring)
Note: The spring night is somewhat sensual, while the autumn night is solitary or lonely.

カーテンの二重に垂るゝ朝寝かな

kâten no nijûni taruru asane kana

window curtains—
a double layer
for sleeping in

Seasonal word: sleeping in (spring)

シクラメン人を恋ふ夜の眉蒼し

shikuramen hito wo kou yo no mayu aoshi

cyclamen—
longing for him tonight
I shave my eyebrows

Seasonal word: cyclamen (spring)

夏に入るや瞼の裏に海生まれ

natsu ni iru ya mabuta no ura ni umi umare

entering summer—
behind my eyelids
the sea is born

Seasonal word: entering summer (summer)

恋したや苺一粒口に入れ

koi shita ya ichigo hitotsubu kuchi ni ire

longing for love—
I place a single strawberry
in my mouth

A red and round strawberry reminds me of my first love. After such a long time, it might sound strange to think about first love, but sometimes I have this mischievous temptation to fall into a new love.

Seasonal word: strawberry (summer)

梅青し女のもてる悪だくみ

ume aoshi on'na no moteru warudakumi

plums so green—
a woman embracing
a malicious design

Seasonal word: plum (summer)

黴の宿いくとせ恋の宿として

kabi no yado ikutose koi no yado toshite

mildewed rooms—
for how many years these rooms
as our love nest

This apartment house with two rooms and a dining kitchen had been my fort and at the same time a place for ease. When I come back here at night and light the room, I feel my body and my mind winding down. It also has a history of being our love nest for a long period of time.

Seasonal word: mildew (summer)

心病む日なり藤椅子にふかくゐて

kokoro yamu hi nari tôisu ni fukaku ite

heartsick day—
nested deeply
in the rattan chair

Seasonal word: rattan chair (summer)

夏帯や一途といふは美しく

natsuobi ya ichizu to iu wa utsukushiku

summer kimono sash—
to live with all one's heart
is beautiful

Seasonal word: summer kimono sash (summer)

死ねぬ髪手に梳きあまる蛍かな

shinenu kami te ni suki amaru hotaru kana

unable to die
I comb the mass of hair in my hand . . .
fireflies

How many times in lifetime do we think dying? No matter how seriously we think, we cannot kill ourselves so easily when the time comes. It is said that the less happy a woman is the greater the volume of hair she has.

Seasonal word: firefly (summer)

女一人目覚めてのぞく螢籠

on'na hitori mezamete nozoku hotaru kago

a woman alone—
she wakes up and peeks into
the firefly cage

In the season of fireflies, I always hang a firefly cage. Their lives are so fragile that I can not help checking them every morning. When I find a firefly lying at the bottom of the cage, my heart sinks for the morning.

Seasonal word: firefly (summer)

愛たしか夏蝉朝を奏でけり

ai tashika natsuzemi asa wo kanade keri

true love—
summer cicadas play
a morning tune

Seasonal word: summer cicada (summer)

青き青き落ち梅踏みぬけふ逢はむ

aoki aoki ochi ume fuminu kyô awan

green green
a fallen plum I stepped on—
I yearn to see him today

Seasonal word: Japanese plum (summer)

54

滝の音に言葉とられし涼しさよ

taki no ne ni kotoba torareshi suzushisa yo

our spoken words
carried away by the waterfall—
coolness!

Seasonal word: waterfall (summer), coolness (summer)

夜濯の己れ独りのものばかり

yosusugi no onore hitori no mono bakari

washing at night—
all the laundry
is my own

Seasonal word: washing at night (summer)

わが掬めば泉涸るゝか罪数多

waga kumeba izumi karuruka tsumi amata

when I draw water
will the spring run dry?
so many sins of mine

Seasonal word: a spring (summer)

渇癒す泉に罪の顔写し

katsu iyasu izumi ni tsumi no kao utsushi

quenching my thirst—
a sinner's face reflected
in the spring

Seasonal word: a spring (summer)

朝顔やすでにきのふとなりしこと

asagao ya sudeni kinô to narishi koto

morning-glory—
already it belongs
to yesterday

Seasonal word: morning-glory (autumn)
Note: Masajo was longing desperately for it. And now it is over and the
day has passed. Every moment of it has become something of the past.
Yet every moment is still vivid in her mind. A morning-glory of yester-
day will never bloom again.

朝顔は実に倖せは小さきに足る

asagao wa mi ni shiawase wa chisaki ni taru

morning-glory
the small promise of its seeds
is sufficient

*I will not set my hopes too high. This humble happiness at hand now is what I
must treasure. The morning-glory that bloomed every morning is bearing seeds
now. I will gather them for next year to grow the beautiful flowers again.*

Seasonal word: morning-glory (autumn)

白桃に人刺すごとく刃を入れて

hakutô ni hito sasu gotoku ha wo irete

into a white peach
like stabbing someone
the knife's edge

Seasonal word: white peach (summer)

わが恋や秋風渡る中に在り

waga koi ya akikaze wataru naka ni ari

my love—
the autumn wind
carries it on

Seasonal word: autumn wind (autumn)
Note: Mosajo's love had continued for forty years. The love has become
old, but it is still hale in the autumn wind.

裏切るか裏切らるゝか鵙高音

uragiru ka uragiraruru ka mozu takane

shall I betray him
or let him betray me?
the shrike's shrill cry

There was once a time of difficulty. I thought of breaking faith with him before
he did it to me but nothing happened after all.

Seasonal word: shrike (autumn)
Note: *Mozu* (shrike) is an autumn *kigo* (seasonal word). The bird has a
very sharp voice and its voice is often made into haiku. It is also
famous for the way in which it stores its prey. *Mozu* catches insects and
frogs and skewers them on twigs.

芒野に心の責苦捨てに出づ

susukino ni kokoro no semeku sute ni izu

field of pampas grass—
I go there to cast away
the anguish of my heart

Seasonal word: field of pampas grass (autumn)

枯草のひと思ふとき金色に

karekusa no hito omou toki konjiki ni

withered grass
when I think of him . . .
burnished gold

The bank of the Imperial Palace was withering beautifully. When I saw it, his image flashed in my mind. My heart beat faster and the withered grass began to glow a golden color.

Seasonal word: withered grass (winter)

枯芝の黄も目に痛し背きたり

kareshiba no ki mo me ni itashi somukitari

withered grasses' yellow, too
pains my eyes—
I have betrayed

Seasonal word: withered grass (winter)

冬の夜の鏡にうつるものにわれ

fuyu no yo no kagami ni utsuru mono ni ware

winter night
things reflected in the mirror
including myself

I unlock the door of my apartment house, and switch on the light. The face I find in the vermilion-lacquered three-sided mirror shows real solitude, unlike the cheerful one I wear at work in my pub. My true self.

Seasonal word: winter

雪清浄黒手袋をもて掬ふ

yuki seijô kuro tebukuro wo mote suku'u

pure snow—
I scoop it up
with black gloves

Seasonal word: snow (winter)

さびしさの雪掬ふとききはまるか

sabishisa no yuki suku'u toki kiwamaru ka

loneliness . . .
as I scoop the snow
it overcomes me

Seasonal word: snow (winter)

風立つとかなしびあへり雪の樹々

kaze tatsu to kanashibi aeri yuki no kigi

when the wind blows
they share their sorrow—
trees covered with snow

Seasonal word: snow (winter)

雪の夜の荒れし唇拭ふかな

yuki no yo no areshi kuchibiru nugu'u kana

my chapped lips . . .
I smooth them
on a snowy night

Seasonal word: snow (winter)

冬の夜の海眠らねば眠られず

fuyu no yo no umi nemura neba nemura rezu

a night in winter—
unless the sea can slumber
I too am sleepless

As the night deepens the surf sound gets into my ears and I can not fall asleep.
People do sleep at night, but the sea does not. I will stay awake with the sea;
the sea is alive.

Seasonal word: a night in winter (winter)

冬の波いまわれのみに寄するかな

fuyu no nami ima ware nomi ni yosuru kana

winter surf
now it dashes against
me alone

Seasonal word: winter surf (winter)

YÛBOTARU
(EVENING FIREFLY)
1976

独語またおのれ慰む春の雪

dokugo mata onore nagusamu haru no yuki

talking to myself
consoling myself once more . . .
snow in spring

Seasonal word: snow in spring (spring)

かのことのもしも還らば暖し

kano koto no moshi mo kaeraba atatakashi

that memory
if it comes to life again . . .
warmth within me

Seasonal word: warm (spring)

おぼろ夜やアパートの鍵店の鍵

oboroyo ya apâto no kagi mise no kagi

hazy night—
the key to my apartment house
the key to my pub

Seasonal word: hazy night (spring)

梅雨ふかし見えざる糸を誰が引く

tsuyu fukashi miezaru ito wo dare ga hiku

deep plum rain—
this invisible string
who is pulling it?

Seasonal word: deep plum rain (summer)
Note: *Tsuyu* (plum rain) is a rainy season in Japan, starting in early June (May in the lunar calendar) and continuing into the middle of July. In the first half of the season, it rains gently, almost like drizzling. In the latter half, there are often downpours. Japanese plum trees bear green fruits in this season.

蛍籠見られて悪き手紙も来ず

hotarukago mirarete waruki tegami mo kozu

firefly in a cage—
clandestine letters
come no more

Seasonal word: firefly (summer)
Note: While Masajo stayed in her marriage, she received secret letters
from her lover. Now she is out of that marriage, there are no more such
letters, nor such excitement.

ある夜ひとり泣いて額まで夏布団

aru yo hitori naite nuka made natsubuton

that night sobbing alone—
up to my forehead
in the summer sheets

Seasonal word: summer bedclothes (summer)

人は盗めどものは盗まず簾巻く

hito wa nusumedo mono wa nusumazu sudare maku

I have stolen a man
but never a thing of value
I roll up the bamboo blind

Seasonal word: bamboo blind (summer)

白玉や愛す人にも嘘ついて

shiratama ya aisu hito nimo uso tsuite

sweet rice dumplings—
even to my love
a little white lie

This is one of my favorite haiku. I fibbed and he knew it well. This happened one day—the cute fib of a woman.

Seasonal word: sweet rice dumplings (summer)
Note: *Shiratama* is a rice-flour dumpling chilled and served with brown sugar syrup, a popular summer sweet. The white of the *shira* (white) *tama* (ball-shaped thing) is very refreshing in the heat.

悔なき生ありやビールの泡こぼし

kui naki sei ari ya bîru no awa koboshi

without regret . . .
is such a life possible?
beer foam overflowing

I can say I do not have any regrets, but deep in my mind it remains like a precipitate. Is there anyone who lives and has no regrets? The death of my ex-husband makes my heart suffer from remorse.

Seasonal word: beer (summer)

夕焼や若し夫在らば厨妻

yûyake ya moshi tsuma araba kuriyazuma

evening glow—
I would be in the kitchen
for my husband

Seasonal word: evening glow (summer)

天の川こころ乾けば髪洗ひ

amanogawa kokoro kawakeba kami arai

river of heaven—
my heart so parched
I wash my hair

Seasonal word: river of heaven, the Milky Way (autumn)

女の秋髪染めあげてうらがなし

on'na no aki kami someagete uraganashi

woman's autumn—
as I finish dying my hair
heartache seeps in

First it was every three months that I dyed my hair; now it is every month.
And within a few days, I find some gray parts coming out near the temples . . .

Seasonal word: autumn

こほろぎやある夜冷たき男の手

kôrogi ya aru yo tsumetaki otoko no te

crickets—
the man's hands
cold on that night

Seasonal word: cricket (autumn)

萩に風鳴りこの溜息は気どられず

hagi ni kaze nari kono tameiki wa kedorarezu

the wind whistles
through the bush clover—
my sigh unheard

My pub is going well, and I am getting out of debt gradually. My life is like clockwork: I go to work every day, repeat the same work, and return home at the same time. If I complain that this life is too ordinary, commonplace, I will be punished.

Seasonal word: bush clover (autumn)

鵙に目覚め旅とても髪乱すまじ

mozu ni mezame tabi totemo kami midasumaji

waking to a shrike's cry—
on this journey my hair
never in disarray

Seasonal word: shrike (autumn)

女体冷ゆ仕入れし魚のそれよりも

nyotai hiyu shi'ireshi uo no sore yorimo

my woman's body
colder than the fish
I keep on hand

Seasonal word: cold (autumn)

冬靄の彼方や抱くも抱かれしも

fuyumoya no kanata ya daku mo dakareshi mo

winter mist—
memories of embracing
and being embraced

Seasonal word: winter mist (winter)

寒紅や心の闇は覗かれず

kan beni ya kokoro no yami wa nozokarezu

midwinter rouge—
my heart's darkness
cannot be discerned

Seasonal word: midwinter rouge (winter)
Note: Rouge made from safflower in this season was said to be of the
highest quality and was treasured by aristocrats in Kyoto since long
ago.

IMACHIZUKI
(18TH DAY MOON)
1986

居
待
月

来し方は霞の奥に隠したし

koshi kata wa kasumi no oku ni kakushitashi

my past—
I wish it could be hidden
deep in the mist

Seasonal word: mist (spring)

引鴨のその先々のことは知らず

hikigamo no sono sakizaki no koto wa shirazu

departing geese—
the future
not mine to know

Seasonal word: departing geese (spring)

花冷や箪笥の底の男帯

hanabie ya tansu no soko no otoko obi

cherry blossom chill—
in the bottom of my chest
his kimono sash

Seasonal word: cherry blossom chill (spring)

背信に時効はあらず水を打つ

haishin ni jikô wa arazu mizu wo utsu

a breach of faith
goes on forever . . .
I wet down the walk

Seasonal word: wet down the walk (summer)
Note: *Mizu o utsu* is a summer kigo. People sprinkle water in front of gates, on alleys, and in gardens to get the coolness, usually in the evening.

死にし人別れし人や遠花火

shinishi hito wakareshi hito ya tôhanabi

the one who died
the one who divorced me—
distant fireworks

*My late ex-husband and the man who divorced me, both had strong karmic ties
with me. They were both good men, and I remember only their good sides now.*

Seasonal word: distant fireworks (summer)

背きし夫の墓丹念に洗ひけり

somukishi tsuma no haka tan'nen ni arai keri

my betrayed husband—
I wash his tombstone
with meticulous care

Seasonal word: to wash a tombstone (autumn)

親子とは耳までも似て秋涼し

oyako to wa mimi mademo nite aki suzushi

mother and daughter
alike even to the ears—
autumn cool

Seasonal word: autumn

MIYAKODORI
(BLACKHEADED GULL)
1994

騙されし恋と思はず芝を焼く

damasareshi koi to omowazu shiba wo yaku

deceived in love?
I do not think so . . .
setting fire to the turf

Seasonal word: to set fire to the turf (spring)
Note: In order to kill the harmful insects, fire is set to grass or turf on the
river banks and in the parks in early spring.

灯台の光りの外の猫の恋

tôdai no hikari no soto no neko no koi

outside the lighthouse's
circle of light:
cats' love

Seasonal word: cats' love (spring)

目刺し焼くここ東京のド真中

mezashi yaku koko Tôkyô no do-man'naka

dried sardines
I grill them right here
in the heart of Tokyo

Seasonal word: dried sardines (spring)

おぼろ夜や女も咥へ煙草して

oboroyo ya on'na mo kuwae tabako shite

hazy spring night—
a woman too with a cigarette
between her teeth

Seasonal word: hazy spring night (spring)

働いて作りし花見衣かな

hataraite tsukurishi hanamigoromo kana

fruit of my labor:
this cherry blossom viewing
kimono

Seasonal word: cherry blossom viewing (spring)
Note: Usually the husband buys a kimono for his wife, but Masajo
earned her kimono for cherry blossom viewing by working in her pub.
Cherry blossom viewing kimonos are usually very fancy and expensive,
and can cost one million yen (about $10,000) or more. Here Masajo
shows her pride.

隠しごと親子にもあり桜餅

kakushigoto oyako nimo ari sakuramochi

secrets come between
even mothers and daughters—
cherry blossom cakes

Seasonal word: cherry blossom cake (spring)
Note: Cherry blossom cake is a cake wrapped in a salted cherry leaf; it is
a specialty of the spring season. It is usually pale pink like cherry
blossoms and its cherry leaf flavor is favored by many people.

日脚伸ぶ身をすり合ひて金魚の恋

hiashi nobu mi wo suriaite kingyo no koi

lingering daylight—
two bodies snuggle
goldfish in love

Seasonal word: lingering daylight (spring)

春愁を抱くほど花を買ひにけり

shunshû wo daku hodo hana wo kai ni keri

spring sorrow—
I buy enough flowers
to embrace it

Seasonal word: spring sorrow (spring)

運やつと向いて来し桃咲きにけり

un yatto muite kishi momo saki ni keri

fortune at last
comes my way—
peach trees blooming

Seasonal word: peach blossom (spring)

春愁の顔となる眉引きにけり

shunshû no kao to naru mayu hiki ni keri

spring sorrow
revealed on my face
as I trace an eyebrow

Seasonal word: spring sorrow (spring)

わが衣白き牡丹と昏れ残る

waga koromo shiroki botan to kure nokoru

my kimono
and the white peony
linger in twilight

Seasonal word: peony (summer)

死なうかと囁かれしは蛍の夜

shinouka to sasayakareshi wa hotaru no yo

shall we die together?
he whispers in my ear . . .
fireflies at dusk

Seasonal word: firefly (summer)

恋を得て螢は草に沈みけり

koi wo ete hotaru wa kusa ni shizumi keri

firefly finds his love
they settle into grass
together

Seasonal word: firefly (summer)

恋遂げし蛍ゆつくり夜明け待つ

koi togeshi hotaru yukkuri yoake matsu

love fulfilled . . .
fireflies leisurely await
the sunrise

Seasonal word: firefly (summer)

蛍火の青くなければ情湧かず

hotarubi no aoku nakereba jô wakazu

firefly light—
unless it is blue
passion won't spill out

Seasonal word: firefly light (summer)

女より買ひし恨みや蚊喰鳥

on'na yori kaishi urami ya kakuidori

a woman's hatred
is what I have invited—
bats flying

Seasonal word: bat (summer)

短夜や嫌ひな人も夢に佇ち

mijikayo ya kiraina hito mo yume ni tachi

short night—
also someone I dislike
in my dream

Seasonal word: short night (summer)

人は人恋ひ秋の蛍は水を恋ふ

hito wa hito koi aki no hotaru wa mizu wo kou

people love people
autumn fireflies long
for water

Seasonal word: autumn

今生のいまが倖せ衣被

konjô no ima ga shiawase kinukatsugi

in this life
the happiest moment now:
boiled baby taros

I believe that now is the happiest time in my life.

Seasonal word: boiled taros (autumn)
Note: *Kinukatsugi* is a boiled baby taro in its skin. *Kinu* means "kimono"
and *katsugi* means "to wear," so it is a taro in its kimono. When pressed
between the fingers, the skin comes off easily, like taking off one's robe.
The dish has been a typical offering for the moon-viewing ceremony. It
is also a favored dish at pubs and at home in autumn, eaten with a
sprinkle of salt.

亡き人へ嫉妬いささか萩括る

naki hito e shitto isasaka hagi kukuru

he's passed away but
a little jealousy remains—
I bind the bush clover

Seasonal word: bush clover (autumn)

秋風や裸足の爪の貝と化し

aki kaze ya hadashi no tsume no kai to kashi

autumn breeze—
the nails on my bare feet
become sea shells

Seasonal word: autumn breeze (autumn)

砂噛んで果つるほかなし秋の波

suna kande hatsuru hoka nashi aki no nami

dashing against the sand
an unavoidable end—
autumn surf

Seasonal word: autumn surf (autumn)

恋の矢の的はづしけり秋の風

koi no ya no mato hazushi keri aki no kaze

love's arrow
has missed its mark—
autumn wind

Seasonal word: autumn wind (autumn)

どうしても落葉踏まねば行けぬ路

dôshitemo ochiba fumaneba yukenu michi

no escaping it—
I must step on fallen leaves
to take this path

Seasonal word: fallen leaves (winter)

過去は運にけふは枯野に躓けり

kako wa un ni kyô wa kareno ni tsumazu keri

once on my fate
today in the withered field
I stumble again

Seasonal word: withered field (winter)

泣き黒子育てて泣かぬ牡蠣を割る

nakibokuro sodatete nakanu kaki wo waru

a mole under my eye:
I nurture it and split an oyster
that does not cry

Seasonal word: oyster (winter)
Note: It is said that if one cries a lot, a mole under one's eye grows
darker or becomes more visible. Therefore one who has a mole in this
spot is said to live a tearful life. Masajo's sorrow makes her think she is
growing a mole.

遠き遠き恋が見ゆるよ冬の波

tôki tôki koi ga miyuru yo fuyu no nami

distant distant love
is something I can fathom . . .
winter surf

Seasonal word: winter surf (winter)

冬の滝音を殺して落ちにけり

fuyu no taki oto wo koroshite ochi ni keri

waterfall in winter—
it quiets itself
and falls

Seasonal word: waterfall in winter (winter)

冬の旅香水はシャネル五番を持ち

fuyu no tabi kôsui wa shaneru go ban wo mochi

winter journey—
the perfume I carry
is CHANEL No. 5

Seasonal word: winter

霧氷林をんな汚れしごとく佇つ

muhyôrin on'na yogoreshi gotoku tatsu

frost-rimed forest—
a woman as if unchaste
stands still

Seasonal word: frost-rimed forest (winter)

夜の雪聡き獣の耳持たず

yoru no yuki satoki kemono no mimi motazu

night snow—
the keen ears of beast
are not mine

Seasonal word: snow (winter)

不機嫌の二つ割つたる寒卵

fukigen no futatsu wattaru kan tamago

in a bad temper
I break two:
midwinter eggs

Seasonal word: midwinter (winter)
Note: Midwinter eggs are laid during the midwinter period, which
happens to be the hen's natural laying-period, so the eggs are very
nutritious. The bright yellow yolk makes the people associate it with
light or flame, and it brightens their heart in the cold weather.

SHIMOKUREN
(PURPLE MAGNOLIA)
1998

春の夢覚めてあしたもこの夢を

haru no yume samete ashita mo kono yume wo

spring dream—
I come out of it and tomorrow
this dream again

Seasonal word: spring

恋失せて蝶のもつれを見てをりぬ

koi usete chô no motsure wo mite worinu

love is gone . . .
entangled butterflies
in front of me

Seasonal word: butterflies (summer)

落椿罪ある者を通せんぼ

ochi tsubaki tsumi aru mono wo tôsenbo

fallen camellias—
barring the way of someone
who has sinned

Seasonal word: camellia (spring)
Note: The most commonly seen camellias in Japan are the red ones.
When a blossom falls, it falls as a whole, rather than petal by petal. In
the *samurai* culture, they were associated with bloody, cut-off heads, and
hence were not appreciated. However, white camellias are very much
favored in tea ceremony culture.

蛍をいのち預けし人とみる

hôtaru wo inochi azukeshi hito to miru

fireflies—
the man I trust my life with
we gaze together

Seasonal word: firefly (summer)

浴衣着て闇夜月夜と逢ひつづけ

yukata kite yamiyo tsukiyo to ai tuzuke

in our yukata—
inky nights moonlit nights
are all for love

Seasonal word: yukata, an informal cotton kimono (summer)

祈ること知らぬ女に星流れ

inoru koto shiranu on'na ni hoshi nagare

for a woman
unable to pray . . .
a falling star

Seasonal word: falling star, shooting star (autumn)

かのことは夢まぼろしか秋の蝶

kano koto wa yume maboroshi ka aki no chô

were they dreams
or were they illusions—
autumn butterfly

Seasonal word: autumn butterfly (autumn)
Note: 'Kanokoto' refers to the nights of love.

草の花遠き記憶の甦り

kusa no hana tôki kioku no yomigaeri

grass flowers—
distant memories
return to me

Seasonal word: grass flowers (autumn)

天高く持つて貰ひし旅鞄

ten takaku motte moraishi tabi kaban

lofty sky—
my love carries
my travel bag

Seasonal word: towering sky (autumn)
Note: *Tentakashi* is an autumn *kigo* (seasonal word) of the sky seen so
high in the clear and crisp air. This feeling is particular to late October
in Japan.

濡れ砂に愁思の手形押しにけり

nuresuna ni shûshi no tegata oshi ni keri

autumn meditation—
a hand pressed into
wet sand

Seasonal word: autumn meditation (autumn)

秋風に拾ひし貝の名は知らず

aki kaze ni hiroishi kai no na wa shirazu

autumn wind—
I picked up a shell
its name unknown

Seasonal word: autumn wind (autumn)

人声のうしろより来る野分かな

hitogoe no ushiro yori kuru nowaki kana

someone's voice
from behind me . . .
autumn gale

Seasonal word: autumn gale, field dividing wind (autumn)
Note: *Nowaki* is the high, violent wind that blows a path through the
grass in autumn. After it is gone, there are broken bamboo fences and
chopped chrysanthemums in the clear and crisp air.

初日の出待つときめきは恋に似て

hatsu hi no de matsu tokimeki wa koi ni nite

first sunrise—
I wait with a fluttering heart
as if in love

Seasonal word: the first sunrise (the New Year)

読初の男が留守を預かりぬ

yomizome no otoko ga rusu wo azukarinu

first reading—
while I am away from home
it's all he does

Seasonal word: the first reading of the year (the New Year)

雪女恋の手管は知りつくし

yuki on'na koi no tekuda wa shiri tsukushi

Snow Lady—
the wiles of love
are her domain

Seasonal word: Snow Lady, Snow Fairy (winter)
Note: The Snow Lady is a snow fairy who appears on heavily snowing
nights in a white kimono.